Hell, Bring the Kids Too
by Megan Ulrich

I think Heaven is complete silence
or maybe that's Hell.
It's been hard to tell the difference lately.

Dedication

For Asher and Rowan, whose souls have made my life worth living.

For my JoeJoe, you will always be my safe place to land.

And for my generative and merciful Father, Thank You.

Contents

* "Third Planet" was inspired by the Modest Mouse song of the same name.

Moving Day

I've been up for thirty minutes,
but I refuse to detach
myself from the negative space
I've burrowed into your body.
It took me all night to find
just the right spot.

Our life is piled around us in
eight cardboard boxes that can't seem to
contain the last two hundred and
fifty-five days of our life.

That first night, getting used to the
way your body felt next
to mine.

When I vomited twelve
times in two days and you built
me a fort out of gas station Mexican
blankets and fed me off-brand
pedialyte that tasted like absolute
shit.

The day I proudly held a pee
stick in the air and we kissed and
danced in the most beautiful silence
I've ever heard.

Do you remember when our life could
fit in a single bedroom and our problems
were contained to three hundred and
fifty square feet of sex and tears
and yelling and soft kisses I could
barely feel with my eyes?

Third Planet

We're two people winding in and out of each other's lives.
When do we become one? Maybe I missed it,
between the people shouting congratulations and
this is the best day of your life.

No one told me how to wake my husband
up at 2 am and tell him the wetness he feels
is blood and that our world is over.

They never told me what to do with unused
onesies or how to hide our future in this
tiny house.

Sometimes it feels like I can't breath and
I haven't moved from this bed since August,
not really anyway. Neither have you.

But we'll stick to the same well-worn arguments about
whether it's better to run or walk in the rain and ignore
the atmosphere caving in around us.

Strawberries

It's really very cold outside
but I want it to be spring so badly
I refuse to turn on the heat for fear
it might scare away the sun.

It's only been three hours since you
left, but it feels much longer than that.
You'll be back in seven hours and then
we'll eat and talk and sleep and
do it all over again tomorrow.

I keep trying to fill these hours between
the times you come and go from
our bed that keeps getting smaller
and smaller as our family grows
larger and larger.

Last summer while picking strawberries
I met a tired beautiful woman who seemed
to be just fine placing her freshly picked
berries in a basket she fashioned with
the bottom of her t-shirt.

I couldn't help but stare at the stretch marks
she proudly bore on her stomach
even though they felt too intimate for me to see.
They seemed to define her in a way I never fully
understood until now.

I'm tired of wearing these clothes that
don't ever seem to fit and the feeling of shame
I have when you slowly take them piece by
piece off my body.

And then she kicks me hard in the
gut and for a moment this silence is
filled with my laughter and everything
is still hard, but it's bearable.

Maybe that will be me one day,
picking the last batch of strawberries
for our tiny wooden kitchen table,
using an old t-shirt to make sure
I've gotten every last one.

Maybe I've Forgotten

How the words hurl out of
        my body in such fragmented
                pieces
sometimes they never find their way
back.

Maybe I've forgotten what it feels like
        to be known.

Maybe it's time to let go of that.

Birthday Party

My best friend
just called me from
New Zealand,

sitting in a port-a-potty
stealing wifi from a hostel
while drinking shitty booze
on his brother's birthday
because someone should
be celebrating.

For the past four months
he's been living in a one man
tent that's too big and
his meals consist of rice and
beans and he's sad in a way
that makes me question
happiness.

And sometimes I wonder
why I'm here worrying about
paint samples and overdue
library books and rashes
on my toddler's leg.

Maybe I should be
doing something beside changing
diapers and growing sourdough
on my counter like it's a goddamn
pet.

And sometimes I just wonder why
I'm here.

Asher

but you
my son

have been a choice/ from the beginning
      I fought for you
      advocated for you
      pumped breastmilk for you
but I haven't gotten lost in you
      haven't fallen into your eyes
instead I analyze you
      scan your body for breathing
            feel for the reassuring pulse I've seen on
monitors since before you were born
you are systolics, and the fear of retinopothy, and low flow
oxygen
you are serfactin and bradycardia and HELP HELP my son is
turning blue
you are *you're young and this child might not be viable- you have
options*
you are a three-minute hand scrub and the smell of hospital
grade sanitizer
you are I'm afraid to touch him
      I'm afraid to hold him
      I'm afraid

you are waking up with a cold sweat because I thought it was
you they airlifted to Vanderbilt, not the
child whose parents are planning a funeral instead of a
baptism
you are a blessing and a joy and
        you absolutely terrify me

but you
my son

I will keep choosing you

One Bread, One Body

I want the distance back,
but the space between
you and I
has been dwindling.
Sometimes I wonder
if there really are miles between
our heads,
throbbing from the tears that won't go away.
I want to go back to when
you were you
and
I was me
and I didn't mourn for mothers I've never met.
Maybe these callouses will grow soon enough.

Harper

My dog has separation anxiety
which is really just a fancy way of saying
my dog is high maintenance
which is really just a nice way of saying
I hate my dog.

But I love my husband
and my husband loves my dog
so I bring her everywhere:
to the store, the park, the library,
and I feed her trazodone and
prozac from a peanut butter spoon
and play her classical music and
I feel like "that woman" who cares
about her dog wayyyyyy too much.

But I love my husband
and my husband loves my dog
so we go to the pharmacy
to fill her prescriptions and
we work on different relaxation
techniques and sometimes I feel
like I'm babysitting a depressed middle-aged
housewife who drinks one too many glasses
of red wine with dinner.

Because if we leave her too long she feels
trapped and tries to escape
but her head gets caught in the bars of the crate and
if I don't come home quick enough
she'll choke herself and
die.

And I'm not carrying a dead dog
down two flights of stairs because
I know what it's like
when everyone leaves
and it seems like your body can't
fit through the cage they've
trapped you in.

Shots

Two months.
Well really sixty-four days
but who's counting anyway.
I'll never understand why they make
these damn offices so cold.
I can feel how slowly my blood moves through my veins.
A faded monkey smiles at us from
the corner of the room.
You smile too but
you can't see that far.
      Gas maybe.
She walks in the room
hiding the needles in her hand like a secret.
You can tell before the first one goes in
that something is wrong.
For some reason I won't help you this time.
You cry so loud that the air leaves your lungs and
it takes a moment for you to remember
how to breathe.
It's okay.
I forgot too.
Then it's over and before she can put the
teenaged mutant ninja turtle band-aid on your little legs
you're in my arms
and the
whole
world
stops.

Covenant

This isn't what I thought it would be.
Maybe that's trite.
Maybe no one gives a shit, but
somehow the best of us has become the worst and
while the hole in my heart
doesn't seem to be mending,
I'm glad you're here.
        Christ am I glad you're here.

Motherhood

There should be a word
for the moment you realize
you have become everything
you ever hated.

When it's 6 o'clock and your husband
walks in the door and dinner isn't ready
and the laundry hasn't even been started,
but somehow you blame him because
it's better than blaming yourself.
There should be a word for that.

When you're trying to convince your eight
year old to go to karate without his stupid uniform
because it's late and you're too tired to recognize
that you wouldn't be caught dead at a party
without a dress, but somehow his hesitancy is the problem
here.
There should be a word for that.

When your husband sweetly kisses your
neck and even though you aren't asleep
you pretend to be
because it's been too long of a day
to genuinely show affection
to the one person who loves you more than anything.
There should be a word for that.

When you want to tell someone that
you just made mango-applesauce for
your son, but you realize absolutely no one cares
and then, maybe, you wonder why you do.
There should be a word for that.

When it's too late on a school night and your thirteen
year old wants help in algebra, but despite graduating
summa cum laude with a degree in biology,
it's been ten years since you thought about anything but
laundry and meal planning so she
decides to ask her dad, the smart one.
There should be a word for that.

When your 9 month old wakes up way too early
from a nap, but you just want to write one damn poem
so you ignore him for a minute longer than you should.
More than you ever thought you would.
There should be a word for that.

Untitled

And sometimes I want to leave,
but there's nowhere (really) to go

maybe we can run away together.

Pack our lives on our backs
to remember what freedom feels like.

Leave the kids with momo and pa and drive
until we feel our souls again.

Hell, bring the kids too.
They should see the world on fire.

Super Secret Batman Book Club

Our son still yells "dada"
at three o'clock in the morning.
He wants you to read his batman
coloring book even though
there aren't any words.

Every time I go in he
shakes his head and turns away.
He doesn't want me. At least not
right now. He wants daddy to
pick him up in his oversized arms.
I would get so mad
that you were interrupting my precious
sleep for your late-night book club.
You missed him, you said,
and this was your only chance to
hold him.

But you aren't here anymore so
when he yells for you
he gets me instead.
So I try to hold our struggling child until
we fall asleep into each other
and I wonder if I'm fucking him up.
If maybe I shouldn't show him that my
heart is breaking or
that I gave you all my
strength before you lost yours.
Maybe I should cry less
and smile more, but

I'm dreading the day it stops.
The day we both sleep through the night
for the first time
and forget you.

The Ocean

He's been sitting here for half an
hour, taking clumps of dirt in
his stubby fingers and launching
them relentlessly against the tide,
as sure and steady as the waves
that crash into his toes.

With every new onslaught he giggles,
surprised the water reached him again.
Eventually, he stops checking that
I'm still beside him,
focusing solely on his futile mission.

And I can't bear to stop him
so we sit together, silently,
trying to empty the beach of its sand.

About the Author

Megan Ulrich lives with her husband and two sons in a charming little town in East Tennessee. You can find discussion questions for *Hell, Bring the Kids Too* and additional information about the author (including contact information) on her website www.Megan-Ulrich.com.

About the Illustrator

Katie Grugin is a Tennessee-born artist and active duty Army Officer. A mostly self-taught artist, she uses black and white ink drawings in an attempt to understand the beauty of tiny details in the natural world. She currently lives in Oklahoma with her two boxer puppies.

CPSIA information can be obtained
at www.ICGtesting.com
Printed in the USA
LVHW090311090720
660097LV00007B/648

ISBN 978-0-578-53891-4

51099

9 780578 538914

$10.99 USD